Protect Your Business

Protect Your Business

A Small Business Guide to Basic Cybersecurity

Bill Bonney and David Goodman

CISO DRG Publishing
P.O. Box 928115
San Diego, CA 92192-8115
<www.CISODRG.com>
info@cisodrg.com
ISBN 978-1-955976-22-0

DISCLAIMER: The contents of this book and any additional comments are for informational purposes only and are not intended to be a substitute for professional advice. Your reliance on any information provided by the publisher, its affiliates, content providers, members, employees, or comment contributors is solely at your own risk. This publication is sold with the understanding that the publisher is not engaged in rendering professional services. If advice or other expert assistance is required, the services of a competent professional person should be sought.

To contact the authors, write the publisher at the address provided above, "Attention: Author Services."

Artwork by Gwendolyn Peres
Copyediting by Nadine Bonney
Production by Last Mile Publishing

Dedication

I dedicate this book to all the entrepreneurs who have entered the arena with a dream of greatness and a will to make it happen. Without your spirit we'd all still be gathering berries and huddling around fires at night.

Acknowledgments

Thank you to all the CISOs who have given us feedback and encouragement as we've published the two volumes of the CISO Desk Reference Guide. As we expand the CISO Desk Reference Guide Small Business Series, we hope this catalog we are building makes a difference. Thank you to Matt Stamper for his thoughtful feedback on this book. Thank you to my partners, Gary Hayslip and Matt Stamper, for their friendship and collaboration. This journey that we've been on has been even more rewarding than I had hoped!

Nadine Bonney deserves special appreciation as well for painstakingly combing through my word usage disasters and under-appreciation for the Chicago Manual of Style. My most heartfelt thanks to Chris Lawrence at Last Mile Publishing for producing this book and helping us define the look and feel for our catalog.

Finally, I would like to thank the following local small business owners who were kind enough to provide details of their road through security so this book would be grounded in the real world and not just the theoretical ramblings of someone who has lived cyber for decades. Their contributions have helped make Protect Your Business a reality:

Danielle Barger, Jennie Bradach, Tahra Doan, Chris Gluck, Ronn and Lauren Gruer, Jessica Harper, Marinda Neumann, Dr. Irene Nosrati, Leslie Ordel, Dr. Mitchell Shulkin, and Tiffany Torgan.

Thank you as well to Adam Gladsden of Broad Street Labs for his counsel on small business cyber insurance.

Table of Contents

As a small business owner, you wear many hats. Many small businesses use professional firms to provide IT services and security services. However, you still need to be aware and direct the work of those firms. You need to know the questions to ask, you need to know what your requirements are, and you need to sometimes push hard to make sure the necessary services are delivered to you, and you aren't manipulated into buying what you do not need.

Though it takes years of training to become a cybersecurity professional, anyone can take prudent steps to make themselves and their company more secure. In the following eight chapters, I'm going to teach you the basics. I will outline what you need to know to protect your business, yourself, your employees, and your brand from most cybercrime.

There are three fundamental rules I'm going to live by throughout this book.

First, I promise no jargon. I'm going to use plain language to tell you how to become more secure. If I do use a technical term, I'll do so only because you hear it talked about and you need to know what it is. Then I will define it in plain language and tell you what it means to you.

Second, I'm going to be honest about the day-to-day work you need to do to be secure. It's not rocket science, but it does take discipline. That makes sense, right? If it was easy to be cybersecure by buying a product or a service, we'd all be secure by now.

Third, every chapter will come with prudent steps you can take right away to be more secure. I'll tell you what you must do (the basics) and then I'll give you some more advanced advice (intermediate steps and pro steps) so you can take it to the next level. I promise I will not tell you to go do something and then not tell you how.

To say that a lot has been written about cybersecurity since 2011 when the SONY Play Station hack occurred is a vast understatement. Cyber is both sexy and scary at the same time. And while tales of spooks and spies make for good reading, if you're so inclined, most of what we see is scary as hell. By now we all know that every single one of us has been the victim, directly or indirectly, of cybercrime. Our credit card numbers, our personal medical data, and other private information are being leaked or stolen all the time.

Thank you for picking up a copy of *Protect Your Business*.

Introduction

The following eight chapters are divided into two sections. In the first section we focus on securing your business and in the second section we focus on securing your digital brand.

We'll start in Chapter 1 with physical security. It's often overlooked when talking about cybersecurity, but it's critical for your physical protection as well as the first level of protection for cybersecurity.

After physical security, we'll move on to the cyber realm in Chapter 2 and start with awareness. Awareness is critical, both for yourself and to help your entire company prepare for and respond to cybersecurity issues you might encounter.

The next three chapters—protecting your networks, performing updates, and taking backups (Chapter 3), passwords (Chapter 4), and access management (Chapter 5)—address the mechanics of how to secure your company, whether you are a sole proprietor or the leader of your small business.

In Chapter 6 we cover web and social media security, and in Chapter 7 we deal with the very topical and very complex topic of data privacy. In Chapter 8 we dive into the complex world of cyber insurance. In every case, the goal is to make this very consumable. As stated in the preface, the information is presented jargon free. At the end of each chapter, you'll find a series of actions you can take. These are divided into basic, intermediate, and pro steps. Chapter 7 also includes a set of controls and a checklist that you can use to address regulatory requirements for data privacy and, should you need to, qualify for insurance coverage.

Finally, in the Conclusion you'll find a summary of the key advice introduced throughout the book. After you have read, learned, and taken key steps, the Conclusion serves as a reminder to put your new knowledge to regular use. Use this as a catalyst to form the habits that will keep you safe. And when the inevitable breach occurs, look to Appendix A for who to call and what to do to recover.

With that as preamble, let's begin.

Securing Your Business

Introduction

You've probably heard the term "cyber hygiene" and might wonder what it means. It refers to the basic steps we take to keep our systems operating securely. The term cyber hygiene originates from drawing the analogy to personal hygiene, habits we pursue to keep us disease-free and healthy. If maintenance aims to repair problems, hygiene strives to prevent them.

Cyber hygiene should become the habits that we learn as entrepreneurs in the digital age. These are straightforward steps that we take to protect our systems and our data from harm.

In Section 1, we're going to go through these straightforward steps, and I will tell you what you need to do to form the habits you'll need to stay digitally safe and secure.

You can think of this section as teaching you the tools to set up the security layers to protect your valuable digital assets—the devices and data you use to run your business. In Chapter 1, this begins with the physical layer—all security starts with a locked door. You also need to be aware of cyber threats and teach awareness to your employees so you and your employees can better defend your business from cybercrime. Chapter 2 addresses cyber awareness.

Chapter 3 expands the security that started with the physical to your network and your computers and also covers the critical topics of updates and backups. In Chapters 4 and 5, we add another layer of security...managing passwords and controlling who has access to log on to your systems.

At the end of each chapter, you'll find a list of straightforward steps you can take to make your business more secure.

Chapter 1

Lock It Up

Yes, in this book I am talking about cybersecurity, but fundamentally, it is still security. And security starts with simple physical things like doors, locks, and putting records in storage cabinets. One of the most essential actions any business can take is quite simply to lock it up. Of course, I mean more than just locking the front door off hours. Parts of this first chapter may seem very obvious to many of you. I include this narrative for three reasons.

First, one of the easiest cybercrimes to commit is one where the thief already has the account number or, even worse, the password. A thief can get those easily if they (or a confederate) are unsupervised in a room with bank statements, customer records, and computers. Failing to secure a customer's records can be just as devastating as leaving your bank statement out.

Second, discussing this will make access control and other cybersecurity techniques easier to understand. Cybersecurity is still security, and many of the physical security methods we've used for decades can help us be more cyber-secure if we learn how to apply those techniques in our digital lives.

And third, most people don't know how to commit cybercrime. It typically takes specialized training or access to malicious computer code. Yes, some high school dropouts commit cybercrime, but most are trained by someone who knows how to do it. But anyone can snoop through the drawers of your desk or walk out of the office with a laptop computer in a delivery box. The two are, therefore, related. One often leads to the other, and weak physical security increases the chances that a cybercrime will occur.

Layers of Security

Security pros talk about layers of security (or defense in depth). Each layer of security is another door, another lock, or another password. Anything that makes someone stop, take an action, or go around a barrier is another layer.

A simple example of layers of security for a small business is to have an office inside a building with a door and a desk with a lockable file cabinet inside the office. This provides three layers of security. You have a lock on the front door, a lock on the office door, and a lock on the file cabinet. If you consistently put financial records, customer records, and computers under lock and key, confidentiality is protected behind those three layers of security.

Why is this important? Because cybercriminals can get their hands on your sensitive information if they have physical access to your stuff. That's "insider crime." Your disgruntled employee or the cleaning crew could become a threat.

Treat your laptop the same way. Put it in a locked drawer or locked cabinet when you are not there. Be smart about who you trust, and don't give everyone in the company the keys.

As much as we'd like to implicitly trust the people we've hired, especially those who have been with us for years or are family friends, the unfortunate reality is that small businesses experience more than half of all embezzlements.[1] Why? The biggest reason is that small

---

[1] Hiscox embezzlement study:
    https://www.hiscox.com/newsroom/press/hiscox-embezzlement-study.

businesses often lack the safeguards that are commonplace at larger companies.

This lack of safeguards makes small businesses targets. For example, if someone experiences an adverse life-altering event (has a car accident, needs money for rent) and knows no one is watching the proverbial till, the temptation may be too high for that person to resist. Plus, as I'll discuss in the next chapter, bank fraud and the theft of medical records have supplanted credit card fraud in both the number of incidents and dollar impact.

Almost anyone can pull off in-person crime; it just takes an opportunity. One reason people don't commit more crimes is because they would be in physical peril when the offense is committed in person. They can get caught, be arrested, and put in jail.

The alter-ego of in-person crime is cybercrime, which can only be done by those who know how. But cybercrime is usually done remotely, with little to no personal jeopardy. Instead of robbing the till, our miscreant might be tempted to write down account numbers and passwords or take a picture of a customer record with account numbers visible. This may be someone you don't even know. Perhaps they work for the cleaning company or, ironically, the security firm that checks the doors at night.

Besides keeping your possessions safe, multiple layers of security can also help you lower your insurance rates. Your cyber insurance carrier will have several requirements, and your ability to check the box may dictate your rate or even whether you even get coverage.

Shore Up Your Virtual Defenses as Well

In the virtual world, the layered defenses are just as important, and the basics are often called "good cyber hygiene." We'll go into each of these steps in the following chapters, but here is a summary of the key steps to good cyber hygiene that you can take as a small business owner.

Step 1: Stay current with updates. One of the most important layers of digital security is to make sure that the systems you use—computer servers, laptops, smartphones, and tablets, and all the software that turns these collections of metal, plastic, and wires into indispensable tools—are up to date with the latest versions. This especially applies to anything you've just installed because the manufacturing and packaging dates could be months before the ship date. Your first order of business once you install it is to update it.

Step 2: Install protection against malware. Chapter 3 will cover the essential tools to keep your company safe. Protection against malware (viruses and the like) is a critical next step.

Step 3: Implement routine backups. Also in Chapter 3, we're going to go into detail on backups. At a high level, it is essential to ensure you are taking routine backups that are stored somewhere safe and where you can access them in an emergency. Your backups also need to be regularly tested. It is astonishing how many backups are never tested and fail when needed.

Step 4: Set strong, unique passwords and change them regularly. I know you have heard all the warnings about passwords, and we're certainly not saying that managing your passwords is easy. The security industry is working on ways to eliminate passwords. As of this writing, good progress is finally being made, and more companies are using smartphone verification and other means of eliminating the dreaded 13-character mixed-case password. In the meantime, good password management is fundamental to good hygiene. We'll cover this more in Chapter 4.

Step 5: Control access. In Chapter 5, we will cover access control. Ensuring that only the right people can access your critical systems is essential to protecting yourself.

Step 6: Manage your handheld devices. Society has become too dependent on them to leave them at home or off all day. In Chapter 3, I'll review essential handheld device hygiene.

Step 7: Train your employees. You have probably heard it said that your employees are your first line of defense and your Achilles' heel, often in the same breath. What is true in the physical world is equally true in the digital world. Your employees must know what to do with spam and phishing emails, when to alert you about unusual activity, and how to handle sensitive customer information to protect the customer's privacy and keep you out of regulatory trouble. An employee training program is even mandated in some industries.

In the next chapter I will help you make these kinds of crimes even less likely, but for now, here is a summary of the key steps we've covered to help you physically secure your business.

Basic Steps

- Clear your desk of any financial documents or client/patient records when you are not in your office and put them in locked storage cabinets when the office is closed

Intermediate Steps

- Make sure everything valuable is behind three layers of security

- Be careful who you give keys to and make sure only the most trusted people have all the keys

Pro Steps

- Install security cameras trained on entrances and on valuable assets; if you don't want to watch employees during regular business hours, program them to turn on when closing

- Install a cable lock on high-value assets such as laptops and secure expensive devices so they cannot be carried away easily

Figure 1.1 – Chapter 1 Next Steps

Chapter 2

Cyber Awareness

When we talk about cyber awareness, we're referring to three basic things. The first is general awareness about the topic—what is going on in the world of cybercrime that you need to be aware of to keep your people and your company safe. The second is training your employees to help you keep your company and themselves safe. The third is understanding industry-specific rules, such as merchants needing to protect credit card data and healthcare providers needing to protect patient data.

Let's take them in order.

Cybercrime Awareness

Cybercrime usually starts with a malicious email, either the spam email clogging your inbox or a more targeted phishing email. The job of the email is to plant malware on your system so the crooks can move on to stealing. There are other attacks, but email is easy and cheap and often succeeds, so thieves aren't going to spend more and work harder if they don't have to.

The Scourge of Ransomware

Infecting your computer with ransomware is one common tactic of cybercriminals.[2] In most cases, once ransomware takes hold, the only

---

[2]   The AIDS Trojan, also known as the PC Cyborg Trojan, was one of the earliest examples of ransomware and a notable event in computer security history. It surfaced in 1989 and was created by Dr. Joseph Popp.

reliable way to recover your files is to recreate or restore them from backup. With better backups, companies became more likely to refuse to pay the ransom.

In 2019, ransomware attacks started including a new extortion angle to increase the pressure to pay. The cybercriminals began to steal the files and threaten to release the information if the victim refused to pay. If the criminals have the files, you can do little to combat this issue. The temptation to pay certainly goes up, and each decision is unique. But consider these two factors. First, choosing to encrypt all your sensitive data makes this attack less successful, and second, if you aren't storing data that can damage you when released, you have little to worry about. These are preventive measures, but combined with a good backup scheme, they can make you more resilient to ransomware and ransomware-driven extortion. Chapter 3, Protecting your Network, discusses encrypting files for an extra layer of protection.

It is tempting to assume that because you run a small business, no one is interested in attacking you. Nothing could be further from the truth. Cybercriminals are interested in profiling small businesses to go after payroll, commit wire transfer fraud, steal customer credit card information, medical and dental records, or anything else of value. Small businesses with larger, more well-known customers are also cased because of their access to these potential ransomware targets. This is especially true for suppliers to critical infrastructure, real estate agents, personal assistants, and bookkeepers.

Here is a guide from the FTC that offers advice to protect you against ransomware. As you continue reading this book, you'll learn how to take each of these steps.

RANSOMWARE

Someone in your company gets an email.

It looks legitimate — but with one click on a link, or one download of an attachment, everyone is locked out of your network. That link downloaded software that holds your data hostage. That's a ransomware attack.

The attackers ask for money or cryptocurrency, but even if you pay, you don't know if the cybercriminals will keep your data or destroy your files. Meanwhile, the information you need to run your business and sensitive details about your customers, employees, and company are now in criminal hands. Ransomware can take a serious toll on your business.

HOW IT HAPPENS

Criminals can start a ransomware attack in a variety of ways.

Scam emails
with links and attachments that put your data and network at risk. These phishing emails make up most ransomware attacks.

Server vulnerabilities
which can be exploited by hackers.

Infected websites
that automatically download malicious software onto your computer.

Online ads
that contain malicious code — even on websites you know and trust.

LEARN MORE AT: FTC.gov/SmallBusiness

FEDERAL TRADE COMMISSION

NIST
National Institute of Standards and Technology
U.S. Department of Commerce

SBA
U.S. Small Business Administration

Homeland Security

Figure 2.1 – Ransomware Guide for Small Businesses, Part 1

HOW TO **PROTECT** YOUR BUSINESS

Have a plan
How would your business stay up and running after a ransomware attack?
Put this plan in writing and share it with everyone who needs to know.

Back up your data
Regularly save important files to a drive or server that's not connected to your network.
Make data backup part of your routine business operations.

Keep your security up to date
Always install the latest patches and updates. Look for additional means of protection,
like email authentication, and intrusion prevention software, and set them to update
automatically on your computer. On mobile devices, you may have to do it manually.

Alert your staff
Teach them how to avoid phishing scams and show them some of the common ways
computers and devices become infected. Include tips for spotting and protecting against
ransomware in your regular orientation and training.

WHAT TO DO IF YOU'RE **ATTACKED**

Limit the damage
Immediately disconnect the infected computers or devices from your network. If your data has been stolen, take steps to protect your company and notify those who might be affected.

Contact the authorities
Report the attack right away to your local FBI office.

Notify customers
If your data or personal information was compromised, make sure you notify the affected parties – they could be at risk of identity theft. Find information on how to do that at *Data Breach Response: A Guide for Business*. You can find it at FTC.gov/DataBreach.

Keep your business running
Now's the time to implement that plan. Having data backed up will help.

Should I pay the ransom?
Law enforcement doesn't recommend that, but it's up to you to determine whether the risks and costs of paying are worth the possibility of getting your files back. However, paying the ransom may not guarantee you get your data back.

 LEARN MORE AT: FTC.gov/SmallBusiness FEDERAL TRADE COMMISSION NIST National Institute of Standards and Technology U.S. Department of Commerce SBA U.S. Small Business Administration Homeland Security

Figure 2.2 – Ransomware Guide for Small Businesses, Part 2

These crimes all start in much the same way. It is relatively easy to estimate the size of the prize based on publicly available information you've published on your website or your office location.

Gone Phishing

Armed with information about who they want to target, there are many ways of getting into your systems. Phishing, for example, uses email messages that are more specific than spam to fool people who expect certain types of messages. Perhaps a message that appears to be from a regional bank that runs payroll for customers in a specific region or industry. How about a message that seems to come from a supplier used by many restaurants or bars in the area? These targeted messages work on a surprising number of businesses.

Take It to the Bank

In the past, what we read about most in the news was credit card fraud. However, credit card theft is not as lucrative as it once was. Also, getting money back from credit card companies takes time and effort. Many gangs still do this, but many thieves have also moved on to more lucrative scores by stealing directly from your bank account.

Two major forms of bank fraud affect small businesses. The first is wire transfer fraud, and the second is known as "business email compromise" (also called BEC). Let's talk about wire fraud first. Cyber thieves work hard to get your bank credentials, by which we typically mean user IDs and passwords. They use these credentials to impersonate you online and, with access to your online bank account, can transfer money to another bank using a wire transfer. Typically, this money is transferred outside the country, usually in several hops, or steps, and often to a destination that makes it easy to quickly withdraw funds. The money is then laundered, making it hard to trace and obscuring where it came from. In many cases, these accounts are closed as soon as the money is withdrawn or when it's evident that authorities somewhere are sniffing around the account.

There are several ways to protect yourself from this, even assuming that cyberthieves get your credentials. First, if you do not need to do wire transfers, turn that feature off on your account. Second, make sure that you are at least notified or, even better, that a separate dialog is required with you, perhaps a phone call or a text message, if any features, including wire transfer, are turned off or on. Third, consider a dollar limit for wire transfers from your account. Fourth, require a confirming action, again either a call or text, for any wire transfer. And finally, consider having a second signer on any check or transfer over a specified dollar limit. These steps provide multiple layers of security. They should help you limit the damage that any cyber thieves can do.

Now let's turn our attention to business email compromise. BEC happens when cyber thieves impersonate you in front of your employees. First the cyberthieves case you—they conduct enough reconnaissance to know, for instance, how you typically write emails and what your signature file looks like. They might also watch and learn about what is happening with your business. Armed with this information, they craft an email to an employee that is designed to fool them into wiring money to an account the cyberthieves control.

Assuming your employee was enticed by the email, the safeguards you put in place to combat wire fraud also work here. With no wire transfer feature turned on, your employee can't wire the money. They can't send all of the cash if there is a dollar limit that is below the requested amount. If you are notified or, better yet, your approval is sought first, that acts as a circuit breaker as well.

BEC is usually accompanied by a sense of urgency. BEC works because of the pressure techniques applied. Learning to spot the con allows you to resist the urgency to act, and that's where cyber awareness comes in.

I won't go into the entire world of cybercrime in this book. But one final thought on this topic is that cyberthieves will try to blend in with their surroundings. They will try to take advantage of events, good or bad, scheduled or out of the blue. Just like phone scams for fake charities ramp up when natural disasters occur, so too do cyber scams ramp up around any event in the news. So, be especially vigilant around current emergencies, events, and trends.

Several sources are cited throughout this book for those interested in learning more. Be a good neighbor and share your knowledge with others in your field.

Now that we know the general threat landscape for small businesses, it's time to start thinking about what to do about it.

Stay Informed

With a small business, you have a lot to keep up with, and the time taken from growing your business must not be wasted. Focus only on what you must know to survive. In today's connected world, this includes keeping up with cybersecurity threats. I am not recommending that you become a cybersecurity expert, but to be your own CISO (Chief Information Security Officer), you should keep up on the threats that affect your business. I recommend that you add a small number of tasks to your daily alerts and your weekly routine.

Several excellent sources can help you stay up with the current threats. I recommend the following:

- The Privacy Professor. Rebecca Herold has podcasts (Data Security and Privacy, wherever you get your podcasts), a monthly newsletter and many other resources. Rebecca routinely addresses scams and provides useful tips.
  (sign up here: https://www.privacysecuritybrainiacs.com/)

- BankInfoSecurity Covers topics in risk management, compliance, fraud, and information security: https://www.bankinfosecurity.com/.

- Major publications, such as The New York Times, The Wall Street Journal, USA Today, and likely your local paper run regular articles. The New York Times has a dedicated section with tons of articles. Local papers have dedicated small business features that announce updates to state and local regulations.

- The Federal Trade Commission (FTC) provides an online guide: https://www.ftc.gov/business-guidance/small-businesses/cybersecurity.

- Finally, dedicated security resources such as TechCrunch and Krebs on Security provide regular updates.
  - https://www.techcrunch.com
  - https://www.krebsonsecurity.com

The preceding is not an exhaustive list. The point is that cybersecurity is an important topic of coverage for nearly all publications, and to be up on this topic, you should start reading articles about cybersecurity that apply to businesses in your industry. Focus on those articles in your favorite publications and add one or two of the targeted publications I listed to keep up on cyber threats. Add to that seeking out and focusing on articles about cybersecurity from your favorite industry publication, your regulators, professional associations, and insurance carrier.

Employee Training

Security professionals are fond of saying human hardware (our brains) is the most susceptible to hacking. You can think of social engineering (tricking people into doing things they normally would not) as a branch of hacking that targets the human brain. The truth is we are susceptible and will always be susceptible. We evolved from loose collections of hominids and humanoids that learned to behave in specific ways to survive. Some behaviors are meant to ward off predators, some to prepare for common defense, and others to quickly decide who to trust.

We can't unlearn these behaviors overnight when it took us millions of years to learn them in the first place. We are curious, want to be helpful, are confident when we should not be, and fearful when it is unwarranted. What we need to do to combat our human nature is to automate and train.

Unfortunately, corporate security training has the reputation of being among the most dreaded activities for any corporate citizen. But fortunately, you don't run a large multinational corporation, and you don't have to sit your employees in front of a two-hour video and watch them find inventive ways of not watching it. But you still need to train your employees and keep cyber hygiene at the front of their minds.

There are several good training solutions available, some for free. Anti-malware maker ESET offers a free gamified program, meaning users get badges and certifications as they advance through the program. For many people, that's just enough to make the training palatable.

My suggestion is to make it personal. Help your employees understand how they can be more secure online. Your employees are much more likely to take the training to heart if it makes them feel more personally secure at the same time. Whichever way you deliver the training, ensure it is focused on their security along with yours.

Focus Your Training

With your colleagues and employees, insist that they take care to protect both customer data and the company's sensitive data. Focus on training that targets the following topics:

- Phishing
- Passwords
- Protecting sensitive material
- Cyber-safe behavior

Encourage employees to adopt cyber-safe behaviors, including:

- Apply maximum privacy settings on their social media accounts such as LinkedIn, Facebook, X/Twitter, TikTok, Threads, and Instagram.
- Allow only their contacts to see their personal information, such as birth date and location.
- Use a password manager.
- Always choose two-factor authentication when it is available.
- Lock devices when not in use.
- Inform you immediately if they lose a company-issued device or one is stolen.
- Do not pass around USB (thumb) drives.

Limiting the amount of personal information available online can reduce vulnerability to phishing attacks and identity theft.

In addition to an online training program, how about treating everyone to lunch once a quarter and having a round table discussion? If you can't lead the discussion, find someone who can. I list some excellent resources at the end of the book, including options for connecting with security professionals dedicated to helping make the digital world safer.

An excellent infographic is available from ready.gov. Go to the ready.gov site and search for cybersecurity. They have lots of great material. This full-color PDF can be printed and posted in the lunchroom and other conspicuous places. It can be downloaded from their site as a PDF.

BE PREPARED FOR A
CYBERATTACK

Cyberattacks can lead to loss of money, theft of personal information, and damage to your reputation and safety.

FEMA

FEMA V-1002/June 2018

Cyberattacks are malicious attempts to access or damage a computer system.	Can use computers, mobile phones, gaming systems, and other devices	Can include fraud or identity theft	Can block your access or delete your personal documents and pictures	May target children	May cause problems with business services, transportation, and power

PROTECT YOURSELF AGAINST A CYBERATTACK

Keep software and operating systems up to date.

 Use encrypted (secure) internet communications.

Use strong passwords and two-factor authentication (two methods of verification).

 Create backup files.

Watch for suspicious activity. When in doubt, don't click. Do not provide personal information.

 Protect your home Wi-Fi network.

Figure 2.3 – Cyber-Attack Preparation, Part 1

HOW TO STAY SAFE
WHEN A CYBERATTACK THREATENS

Prevent NOW

Limit Damage DURING

Report AFTER

Keep your anti-virus software updated.

Use strong passwords that are 12 characters or longer. Use upper and lowercase letters, numbers, and special characters. Change passwords monthly. Use a password manager.

Use a stronger authentication such as a PIN or password that only **you would know.** Consider using a separate device that can receive a code or uses a **biometric scan** (e.g., fingerprint scanner).

Watch for suspicious activity that asks you to do something right away, offers something that sounds too good to be true, or needs your personal information. **Think before you click.**

Check your account statements and credit reports regularly.

Use secure Internet communications. Use sites that use "HTTPS" if you will access or provide any personal information. Don't use sites with invalid certificates. Use a Virtual Private Network (VPN) that creates a secure connection.

Use antivirus solutions, malware, and firewalls to block threats.

Regularly back up your files in an encrypted file or encrypted file storage device.

Limit the personal information you share online. Change privacy settings and do not use location features.

Protect your home network by changing the administrative and Wi-Fi passwords regularly. When configuring your router, choose the Wi-Fi Protected Access 2 (WPA2) Advanced Encryption Standard (AES) setting, which is the strongest encryption option.

Limit the damage. Look for unexplained charges, strange accounts on your credit report, unexpected denial of your credit card, posts you did not make showing up on your social networks, and people receiving emails you never sent.

Immediately change passwords for all of your online accounts.

Scan and clean your device.

Consider turning off the device. Take it to a professional to scan and fix.

Let work, school, or other system owners know. Information Technology (IT) departments may need to warn others and upgrade systems.

Contact banks, credit card companies, and other financial accounts. You may need to place holds on accounts that have been attacked. Close any unauthorized credit or charge accounts. Report that someone may be using your identity.

File a report with the **Office of the Inspector General (OIG)** if you think someone is illegally using your Social Security number. **OIG reviews cases of waste, fraud, and abuse.** To file a report, visit www.idtheft.gov.

You can also call the Social Security Administration hotline at 1-800-269-0271. For additional resources and more information, visit http://oig.ssa.gov/report.

File a complaint with the FBI Internet Crime Complaint Center (IC3) at www.IC3.gov. They will review the complaint and refer it to the appropriate agency.

Learn tips, tools, and more at www.stopthinkconnect.org.

Take an Active Role in Your Safety

Go to **Ready.gov/cybersecurity.** Download the **FEMA app** to get more information about preparing for a **cyberattack.**

FEMA

Figure 2.4 – Cyber-Attack Preparation, Part 2

Industry-Specific Regulations

Even though being compliant isn't the same thing as being secure, companies must comply with the security and privacy regulations that apply to them. The most common for small companies include rules for handling credit cards (PCI-DSS) and state regulations protecting personally identifiable information (see Chapter 7 for a more thorough treatment of data privacy regulations) and safeguarding protected health information.

If your firm handles credit cards, as the owner you have signed an agreement with your bank that is mandated by the Payment Card Industry (PCI). You should bookmark the PCI security standards website, which can be found at www.pcisecuritystandards.org. On this site, you will find helpful guides for how to comply with the contract terms. You will also find practical suggestions for awareness training for your employees. Just type "awareness training" in the search box.

These companies also provide excellent training materials and exercises:

- Knowbe4.com – a company that provides privacy training
- ESET.com – anti-malware firm with free employee training

Above all, keep it easy and focus on the minimum number of behaviors you want to change. It's about what your people do, not what they know.

The next chapter, Protecting Your Network, will help you use the tools of the trade that you'll need to secure your business, but for now, here is a summary of the key steps we've covered to help you address cyber awareness and employee training.

Basic Steps

- Add a weekly review of cybersecurity-related articles from your favorite news sources
- Bookmark sites with specific rules for your industry
- Train your employees to resist phishing attacks

Intermediate Steps

- Implement a cybersecurity training program for all employees
- Work with your employees to help them update their online settings to protect their privacy and decrease the likelihood they will be phishing victims
- Secure your bank accounts by limiting or removing wire transfer capabilities

Pro Steps

- Host a monthly or quarterly lunch and learn with your employees to talk about how they can be safer online
- Make sure all money movement requires a second verification step
- Turn on notification whenever changes are made to the features of your bank accounts

Figure 2.5 – Chapter 2 Next Steps

Chapter 3

Protecting Your Network

Talk of firewalls, routers, and networks is very confusing if you don't work with these tools every day. Here is a primer I hope you find helpful.

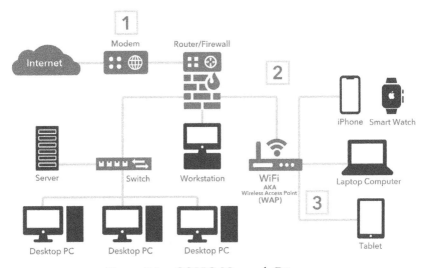

Figure 3.1 – SOHO Network Diagram

I've included a diagram here that depicts a simple SOHO network. SOHO means Small Office, Home Office. I will go through each of these items and describe the protection to have for each. As usual, I'll provide basic, intermediate, and pro steps at the end of the chapter.

Before we dive into the mechanics of safeguarding your systems, performing updates, and taking backups, a great first step is to create an inventory of all the systems (devices, computers, etc.) and applications (email, accounting, inventory control, etc.) you use to run your business. Work with your tech vendor to create this inventory. Ask enough questions to ensure completeness and retain an up-to-date copy that you store safely and can quickly locate. Validate that they account for all the applications and services you use and that they do a network scan to make sure they are aware of every connected device.

Your Perimeter

The portion of the diagram labeled "1" consists of your modem and your firewall, and together, they form a perimeter for your network.

<u>Your modem</u> (digital has mostly replaced dial-up) connects your network to the Internet, typically by way of the phone company or cable company (the carrier).

<u>Your firewall</u> acts as a barrier from your modem to your network by applying rules such as what data types (e.g., email or web traffic) or who (people and programs) to permit into your network.

Update Strategy for Your Perimeter

Your tech vendor should have a regular schedule for performing the recommended firmware and software updates on your perimeter devices. You must make time for these updates, as access to the Internet will be disrupted during this process. However, this can usually be scheduled after hours and is typically a quick process.

Backup Strategy for Your Perimeter

Backups for perimeter devices differ from other devices, often only the configuration changes. Your tech vendor should provide an updated copy of a text file with the configuration settings. Retain a copy of this file somewhere safe, such as on a thumb drive you put in a locked, secure place or on a Google drive or similar cloud storage service.

Your Network

The portion of the diagram labeled "2" includes your router, wireless router (or WiFi router), and a switch (if needed), which for simplicity I'll refer to as your network.

To keep your perimeter and network devices safe, do the following:

Physical security – Keep your modem and firewall out of sight and physically protected. This means off the floor, dry, and relatively cool. Limit access by placing them behind a locked door, such as in a closet.

Device security – These devices often come with rudimentary security turned on. Your tech vendor should change the password or disable all built-in logins to reduce attacks and turn on logging to track changes being made and any access attempts. For your WiFi router, they should also rename it from the default to make it more resistant to attacks.

Electrical power – Work with your tech vendor to implement battery backups for all critical equipment.

Update Strategy for Your Network

Like your perimeter, your tech vendor should have a regular schedule for updating your network devices. I recommend a quarterly cadence, with exceptions for critical updates issued by your devices' manufacturers. This is one of the most important regular maintenance tasks your tech vendor performs for you. Staying diligent with patches is an essential security practice.

This strategy applies to other devices on your network as well. Office equipment, such as printers, occasionally have updates to apply. Also, home and office automation, including lighting systems, security, heating and air, and streaming devices, can require updates. If the system is professionally installed, buying a service plan that includes maintenance and updates is a good rule of thumb. If you installed it yourself, stay informed on the manufacturer's recommendations. Keep in mind that everything is connected; therefore, any device that is not updated is vulnerable to attack and makes your network more vulnerable.

Backup Strategy for Your Network

Although network devices and office automation systems have more complex operating systems than modems and firewalls, as with the perimeter, the backups usually cover just the configuration settings. Having this information readily available can mean the difference between being down for a few hours or a few days. That's time during which you are not running your business. Add your copies of these files to your thumb drive or cloud storage service.

Your Computers

The portion of the diagram labeled "3" encompasses your computing devices, including computers, smartphones, tablets, and other devices. "Devices" does the heavy lifting here and includes connected cash registers and point of sale equipment, smart devices such as smart speakers, wearables, and home/office automation such as lighting, heating and air, appliances, printers, entertainment devices, and security devices such as cameras and motion detectors.

To keep your computing devices safe, do the following:

<u>**Physical security**</u> –All devices should be stored out of harm's way and kept dry and relatively cool. For special-purpose devices, such as cash registers, storing under lock and key when the device is not in use is certainly appropriate. These are valuable items. Consider securing them with a cable lock where possible. Also, do not leave laptops unattended in public places.

<u>Device security</u> – Initial device setup includes some basic security settings, such as setting the boot (power on) password and network settings to allow the device to join your network or your WiFi network. For specialized equipment, have the equipment vendor work with or advise your tech vendor to install and securely configure the devices.

Your Smartphones and Tablets

Never leave your smartphone or tablet unattended or unlocked in public settings. Besides the obvious threat that small portable devices are easy to steal, unlocked devices can provide a trove of information in just seconds or minutes. Set a reasonable timeout for automatic locking of the device. Lock the device manually when not in use. Consider activating facial recognition, fingerprint recognition, or security patterns for added security. Consider activating the security setting that deletes all data at the tenth consecutive incorrect password so that brute force attacks cannot be applied to breaking your security if you lose the device.

Manage your account with your carrier. All major carriers offer two-factor authentication for your mobile account. Use this feature to thwart fraudsters from intercepting your one-time passwords for bank accounts, email, social media sites, etc.

In addition to keeping your device up to date, you should also reboot (power off, power on) your devices regularly. Rebooting helps keep your device running smoothly. Review the privacy settings for your apps, remove apps and files (photos, videos, etc.) you don't need, and delete the files from your deleted photos album. Having at least 20% of your memory available helps your device function properly.

Servers, Workstations, and Laptops

For servers, workstations, and laptops, set the inactive screen timeout to no more than 15 minutes in case you forget to lock the screen when you step away. Set a reasonably complex boot password. By reasonably complex, I mean a minimum of 18 characters with some complexity. This is the one case where you must create a password that you can remember. A phrase is better than a random string of characters. Make your phrase more than 20 characters, and you have a great password. "I won my first game of risk @ 20" is an example of something very easy to remember. It is 32 characters long and has all four character sets represented.

Work with your tech vendor to turn on encryption for your servers, workstations, and laptops. If this is done natively on your device, your boot password becomes your encryption key. If they use a different solution, you must safeguard your encryption key. Losing your key means your will not be able to retrieve any encrypted data.

Work with your tech vendor to ensure you and your employees install and keep anti-virus software updated and configured to provide maximum protection. Include email and browser protection and schedule routine hard drive scans. This is essential. The most common ways to attack systems are through email attachments and poisoned web pages.

Update Strategy for Your Computers

The update strategy for your laptops and workstations must be much more comprehensive. For devices such as phones, tablets, fitness devices, and watches, make sure the operating system is updated whenever new updates come out for the version you have. Your device should notify you, usually as a badge or banner on the device. Also, keep your apps up to date as new versions are provided. Watch for new features and options, and make sure you understand what these new features do for you or to you. Do not be shy about turning off new features until you know how they add value to your daily routine. Every feature represents a security risk. In Chapter 7, I dive deeper into data privacy, and the key takeaway is that every piece of data you leak provides an opportunity for someone to exploit you. So be mindful about what you share and make sure the value you receive in return is worth it.

Your tech vendor must provide similar diligence for your laptops, desktops, and servers. If you are using only general-purpose applications, such as a web browser, word processor, spreadsheet tool, and email, then the likelihood is high that updates will be frequent enough and comprehensive enough to stay up with threats and come with a relatively low risk of causing disruption to your other operations.

If you are using specialized software, such as an accounting package, point-of-sale software, or software that is specific to your industry, you and your tech vendor should stay in touch with the vendor's support staff and follow their instructions for applying updates. Also, keep in mind the suggestions provided below for backups in support of your updates.

Backup Strategy for Your Computers

As with your update strategy, the backup strategy for your computing devices needs to be comprehensive. Starting with your personal devices, you should have local and remote backups for any device that holds your data. By remote backups, I mean backups that are either saved directly to a cloud service or made locally but then sent offsite for safekeeping. Phones and tablets store apps, music, photos, videos, documents, and other data you purchase or generate. These devices should be backed up as the data is specific to you and cannot be restored by reinstalling. Local backups can be achieved by synching your device on a personal computer. Remote backups can be achieved by subscribing to a cloud service. These services are often available from your vendor. For instance, iCloud is available to Apple device owners, as is OneDrive for Microsoft users.

The best practice for your laptops, desktops, and servers, is to have full and incremental backups scheduled monthly, weekly, and daily following the 3-2-1 backup rule. The 3-2-1 backup rule says to keep three backup copies, use at least two different types of media (CD, tape, thumb drive) and store at least one offsite. Your tech vendor should drive this process, but you should have full access to your backups. Take the extra step to verify that new backup files appear when expected, and work with your tech vendor to ensure the integrity of your backups.

A point I just made bears repeating—the best backup strategy is one that works. And it has probably become apparent by now that good systems hygiene is about diligence and caring about the details. As a small business owner, I know you don't have time to obsess over the details, and I know you can't spend any more money on your systems than you must. Spending the time to ensure that your devices are updated, your systems are being routinely backed up, and you can restore your files from backup are among the most important steps you can take to be secure. Consider working with your tech vendor to pick a random device twice a year and verify you can successfully restore that device from a backup.

Smart Speakers, Wearables, and Home/Office Automation

For smart speakers, wearable technology, and home automation such as lighting, heating and air, security devices including cameras, appliances, printers, drones, and entertainment devices, it is tempting to ignore the security concerns because we either don't know much about them or they serve a singular purpose and require little attention to succeed in the mission we have for them.

Work with your tech vendor to configure these devices with the most secure settings that allow you to use them as needed.

Unsecured security cameras and microphone-enabled entertainment devices can be used to spy on their owners. Unpatched networked appliances are routinely commandeered to create botnets that are used to attack the service providers we rely on every day, such as banks, power grids, hospitals, and emergency services. Here are a couple additional steps you can take:

- Enable voice recognition. This sounds counter-intuitive, but by turning on voice recognition, you train your devices to your voice, decreasing the likelihood that another person's voice can seize control of your automation.

- Have your tech vendor configure a guest network for your IoT devices, which includes all the televisions, speakers, lights, wearables, and home/office automation.

In the next chapter, Passwords, I'll show you how to create and use strong passwords, but for now, here is a summary of the key steps we've covered to help you stay on top of updates and backups as a vital step in securing your systems.

Basic Steps

- Always keep your systems in dry, cool, secure places. Keep them up off the floor and out of the line of foot traffic
- Lock all devices
- Change default passwords
- Install and use a firewall and anti-malware software
- Register your devices with the manufacturer to trigger your warranty and be added to routine notifications for updates
- Apply updates for perimeter and network devices as soon as they are available
- Backup all personal devices both locally and using a cloud service

Figure 3.2 – Chapter 3 Next Steps

Intermediate Steps

- Protect your critical systems with a UPS
- Configure your routers and WiFi routers with advanced settings to restrict use outside your network
- Make a backup copy of configuration files for perimeter and network devices
- Periodically check the manufacturer's website for any updates in cases were automatic notification is not available
- Implement a 3-2-1 backup strategy using a backup solution that automates daily, weekly and monthly backup processes

Pro Steps

- Separate WiFi for personal and entertainment devices
- Enable voice recognition and train your devices to recognize your voice
- Make a backup copy before applying updates
- Routinely test your backup strategy by successfully restoring files from the backup copy

Figure 3.3 – Chapter 3 Next Steps (continued)

Glossary

Modem – Modem stands for "modulator-demodulator," which originally meant that it modulated a digital signal from a device to be transmitted over an analog phone line and then demodulated from the phone line back to a digital signal. The modern modem modulates and demodulates between signals of different types.

Firewall – Taken from the physical wall that is often used in construction to provide a barrier to contain potential fire threats, a network firewall limits the data that is allowed from outside to inside a computer network and vice-versa.

Router – A router directs data, also known as network traffic, from one device to another, either across network segments within a network or from one network to another.

Network – A collection of systems that form a cooperative unit within which various resources, such as storage, printers, and data, are shared for a common objective of the users.

Server – Typically a computer that houses or drives shared resources, such as disk drives, printers, tape backup systems and sometimes software, such as accounting, payroll, or customer relationship management (CRM) software.

Workstation – A powerful, single-user computer that is custom-built for specific functions such as CAD (Computer Aided Design), media production, or software development.

WiFi Router – A wireless router that connects to your devices via radio frequency (RF) signals rather than through cables.

Cable Lock – A flexible, heavy-duty, durable cable, often reinforced with metal fibers, that can be used to secure laptops and other portable or movable high-value devices to a building or other immovable structure.

UPS – Uninterruptable power supply. For our purposes these are battery systems ranging from 250 volt-amps (VA) to 600 volt-amps, 900 volt-amps, or as much as 1.5KVA (1,500 volt-amps). In the smaller range, there are probably just the battery and outlets, and in the larger sizes, you'll typically have gauges for load and health and maybe software for configuring alarm signals.

Chapter 4

Passwords

Creating and Managing Strong and Unique Passwords

In Chapter 1, I laid out seven steps for good cyber hygiene. Step 4 is to set strong, unique passwords, and change them regularly. But let's face it, passwords are a pain, and the average person today has more than 100 passwords to manage. I'm not going to give you a long dissertation or fancy mnemonic technique to create an uncrackable password. That is so last decade.

The reality is that short passwords, and by that, I mean anything less than 15 characters, are not secure. For years it was acceptable to say that the computer time required to crack a password of eight, then 10, then 13 characters was measured in the millions or billions of years. But when the prize is big enough, effort and money are deployed. Billions of passwords have been stolen, and techniques have been developed that create tables (called rainbow tables) that act like master keys for any password up to a certain length. It used to be that if you came up with one pretty complex password, you could use it everywhere and be secure. But cyberthieves have a technique called credential stuffing and they use their trove of stolen passwords to try any password of yours they've ever stolen on every system they can think of that you might use.

With all these passwords out there on the black market and techniques to quickly break passwords up to and exceeding 13, 14, even 15 characters, how do you create and maintain more than 100 strong, unique passwords? Forget all those techniques you've learned about substituting numbers for letters and memorizing a nursery rhyme and using the first letter for every word to create passwords. The thieves know these techniques as well. So here are my recommendations for handling passwords:

1. **Use a password manager to create and manage your passwords.** There are several different types of password managers, and some that even allow you to manage the passwords for your company. You can use a cloud-based password manager or one that stores the passwords on your devices.

2. **Use the most secure setting for each account.** If the system you are using does not state its maximum, choose one of at least 18 characters. Also, use the complexity controls to let your password manager set a very complex password when you can.

3. **Don't reuse passwords.** If you allow your password manager to choose your password, this won't be an issue, but don't cheat and reuse a strong password generated for one account on another.

4. **Use unknowable information for your security questions.** The best questions are ones you pick. Create an odd question and make up a bizarre answer and record it in your password manager. If you must use one of their preset questions, simply make up an answer—yes, lie. And then record that answer in your password manager.

A few additional recommendations:

- If you are just starting to use a password manager, focus first on your weak passwords (short passwords, those with simple words, common keyboard combinations) and then hit your sensitive accounts including banks, phones, and email.

- How often you change your passwords depends on the type of account. For financial accounts, try to do it every 90 days.

For others, change it if they disclose an incident, or you notice something suspicious.

- If your password manager has an automatic change option, use it.
- For consumer accounts you use infrequently, consider simply using their password reset feature when you need to log on.

Start your search for password managers by looking up Keeper, LastPass, Dashlane, and 1Password, or use the rating service from CNET magazine (an excellent source of expert advice I rely on) and choose from their Top 10 list. Read the descriptions of the pros and cons and decide what is best for you. Let me leave you with a word of caution. Be careful when searching for software products using Google Chrome. As the most popular browser, Chrome is a favorite target for cyber criminals poisoning search results with malware. Consider using Firefox, Edge, or DuckDuckGo for better security.

Can passwords ever be left behind? There is finally progress being made. Big Tech, including Microsoft, Apple, and Google support something called passkeys on your devices and websites, including Adobe, Amazon, CVS, PayPal, Uber, Shopify, and even TikTok, give you the option to use a passkey to sign in. A passkey is an encrypted certificate on your device that allow you to do a behind-the-scenes handshake with a website rather than providing a user-ID and password. The certificate is protected using biometrics, such as a face scan or fingerprint. As more people adopt passkeys, we might finally be able to retire passwords. Wouldn't that be grand?

In the next chapter, Access Management, I'll talk about how to appropriately grant and limit access to your critical systems, but for now, here is a summary of the key steps we've covered to help you create and use strong passwords.

Basic Steps

- Choose a password manager for yourself and insist that all employees use one that suits them

- Use unique passwords for all accounts, no exceptions

Intermediate Steps

- Subscribe to a VPN service and use it whenever you are not in the home or office

- For financial accounts, change passwords every 90 days

- Make sure all of your passwords are 18 characters or more

Pro Steps

- Use unknowable information for security questions, lie if you can't pick your own questions

- If your password manager has an automatic change option, turn it on for bank accounts

Figure 4.1 – Chapter 4 Next Steps

Chapter 5

Access Management

In Chapter 1 we talked about deciding who needed to have keys to the shop, the office, closets, and drawers, and how to put critical systems behind more than one layer of protection. In this chapter, we're concerned with which users have access to what files and systems and how access is controlled and made safe. There are four main questions to answer about access management:

1. Who do you give access to your systems?
2. What extra steps should you take to secure access?
3. How do you share passwords (when you must) and transfer files securely?
4. What precautions should you take outside your home or office?

Who Do You Trust?

Let's take these in order. Question 1 is "Who do you give access to your systems?"

There are three account types of concern:

1. **User accounts** are the regular accounts that are for employees who need access.
2. **Systems accounts** are accounts that run in the background.
3. **Administrator accounts** are the keys to the kingdom that allow unfettered access to configure and manage the system or application.

It's surprising how many businesses give too many people access to administrator passwords. The combination of feeling overwhelmed by having to make decisions about who gets what access, believing that not having a needed password will slow down employees who are critical to supporting the business, and not really knowing how to set up access correctly can cause us to throw in the towel and just give the administrator passwords to everyone who might conceivably need them.

So, who needs the administrator passwords? Well, as the owner, you need them. If there is a trusted employee who performs many systems administration tasks, that person needs them. And if you have hired a tech vendor, they need them. That's it.

As a small business, you aren't likely to have a lot of system accounts, but the ones you do have are critical and often function out of sight. Make sure you or your tech vendor disables all system accounts that are not in use and changes any default passwords on system accounts you do use. That's an essential step to cut down on the number of ways cyberthieves can attack you.

It is difficult for a small business owner to know what system accounts come with any system they might buy, especially industry-specific software or even general-purpose systems like payroll, customer relationship management, and accounting. This is an area where you will rely on your tech vendor to tune your systems and the applications you use, including in-house and online.

One final recommendation about accounts is to assign everyone a unique account. Don't let people share group accounts unless those accounts are so limited in functionality that they could never be used for anything else.

Here is a simple plan for how to assign accounts:

1. Assign everyone who needs access to computer systems for your company their own, unique user account.
2. Have your tech vendor disable all system accounts you are not using. There should be very few of them and disabling the ones you don't need should be part of the process for setting up a system.
3. Only you and your IT team should ever have access to the administrator accounts.
4. If you do use any shared accounts, and we all know it happens, make sure you change the password when someone leaves. Also see below for a more in-depth conversation about sharing passwords and files.

Who Are You?

Question 2 is "What extra steps should you take to secure accounts?"

The two most critical extra steps to take to secure accounts are to use strong, unique passwords and to use two-factor authentication (2FA) whenever it is available. I covered strong, unique passwords in Chapter 4. Now, let's talk about and demystify two-factor authentication.

Two-factor authentication means having a second factor, like a one-time password (OTP) such as an SMS code or a code from a key fob, authentication app, or smartcard to verify who you are. Besides your password, you provide a second verification method or "factor." That's all it means. The first incarnations of this are familiar to a lot of folks—those tokens or key fobs that some people still carry around that display a code that changes every minute or two.

Now we have a wide range of options, including having a text code sent to your phone, getting a code from an app on your phone (not the same thing as a text code and more secure in most cases), or voice detection when you're calling in to your bank or brokerage. Unlocking an app with your fingerprint or facial scan on your phone or PC is not a second factor. All that does is populate the user-ID and password fields for you, but it still uses the user-ID and password. Biometrics can be used to secure your phone, but unless you use passkeys (as discussed in Chapter 4) it is no more secure online than a user-ID and password combination.

The two-factor technique builds on the idea that someone can easily steal your password, but it's more difficult to steal a physical thing from you (like a phone or key fob) and even more difficult to fake who you are.

Initially, 2FA was mostly used by banks, but now many of the systems and services we use online employ 2FA, and my advice is to use it whenever you can. I suggest you use it for your financial records, your phone, your utilities, and your email account.

Sharing is sometimes more demanding than giving.

- Mary Catherine Bateson

Question 3 is "How do you share passwords (when you must) and transfer files securely?" You have heard it said that you should never share passwords, and we just told you above to give everyone in your company a unique account. But as we also noted, it's sometimes required to share passwords and files. There are safe ways and not-so-safe ways to do it.

Let's deal with sharing passwords first.

Rule 1: Do not do it for mere convenience. Only do it when the cost of not doing so is significant lost productivity, in emergency situations that truly put life, health, or your business at risk, for systems that simply cannot be configured for multiple users, or for low-risk access with many users where the burden of administering the passwords significantly outweighs the security risk.

Rule 2: Change the password whenever any of the following conditions are met:

- You shared the password for a one-time use of the system in question, and that use is concluded.
- Individual(s) within the group that share a password to an asset you protect have left your employment.
- You believe the password has been compromised or see unusual activity.
- You can't remember the last time you changed the password.

Now let's look at sharing files. Again, there are safe ways and not-so-safe ways to share files, and safety should go up in proportion to the sensitivity or value of the data being shared. Documents with unmasked sensitive information, in other words, documents that don't obscure information such as social security numbers, bank account numbers, or personal information about employees, patients, or customers, should never be sent in clear text.

That means don't attach a Word document, Excel spreadsheet, or PDF file to an email message without encrypting the attachment. But encrypting documents is still messy for most users. Therefore, I believe the easiest way to exchange files is with a secure file storage/transfer service. Dropbox, Box, and Citrix ShareFile are all examples, along with Signal, WhatsApp, and Telegram for secure messaging. Again, this is not intended to be an endorsement of any product or service. Consult with your tech vendor for a solution that works for you.

Here are some steps to secure your use of secure file transfers:

- Turn on two-factor authentication.
- Enable email notifications, so you are informed when files are added or accessed.
- Enable logging when available.

- Use a VPN for access (see the next section for VPN information).
- Use strong passwords.
- Delist linked devices you don't need for file sharing.
- Confirm receipt of files you are sharing and delete them once the other party has them.

Don't Leave Home Without It

Question 4 is "What precautions should you take outside your home or office?"

We've heard about how unsafe airport WiFi is and how dangerous it is to connect to the WiFi in the hotel lobby or the local coffee shop. We've heard about Airbnb guests reporting stealth video cameras. Is it safe to travel and use technology? Yes, by taking precautions. The good news is you only need three or four tools to make travel safe.

Let's understand why it is dangerous out there. First, you have no idea what precautions the hotel took when securing their WiFi. Second, public access points, by definition, are open to the public. That means lots of potentially bad actors with unfettered access.

We mentioned three or four tools to make travel safer. These include:

- A VPN – virtual private network for safe use of public access points.
- A USB "charge only" adapter – this device stops unwanted data transfers (e.g., passing a virus to your phone) from occurring over your charging cable when you plug into a public charging station.
- A portable battery pack – a better way to charge your phone on the go is a portable charger you charge up before you leave to give your phone a private boost.
- A WiFi device detector – this is an app you can download and install on your smartphone that allows you to scan any

hotel room, Airbnb rental, or other public place for hidden WiFi cameras or other devices.

A VPN requires you to have an account with a VPN provider but is well worth the cost and trouble if you frequently rely on access while outside the home or office. Using your cellular service instead of public WiFi is a helpful first step but does not entirely protect you as cell towers can be spoofed, meaning a thief can trick your phone into connecting to a fake tower and intercept your traffic.

Use CNET or a similar service or ask your tech vendor to recommend a VPN that meets your needs. A search in your favorite app store should provide you with many options for hidden camera detectors. Again, read the reviews of both consumers and experts before you download an app (especially for Android where the app stores are less curated) to make sure the app is legit. Look up the provider and make sure it is well-rated.

Take a similar approach to battery packs. I suggest getting two, one that is always charging and one you take with you. When you return home, swap them. If you can control the power source, you will not have to worry about plugging into a dirty power port. If you feel you must use a public power port, buy a few USB "charge only" adapters and make sure you always have one with you.

In the next chapter, Web and Social Media Security, we'll talk about how to keep your online presence secure, but for now, here is a summary of the key steps we've covered to help you manage access.

Basic Steps

- Assign every employee their own unique account
- Limit the number of people with privileged or administrator accounts to people with a need to know

Intermediate Steps

- Subscribe to a VPN service and use it whenever you are not in the home or office
- Disable all unused system accounts

Pro Steps

- Bring a battery pack with you and never use a public charging port
- Install a WiFi detector on your smartphone and scan hotel rooms, public spaces and Airbnb rooms for hidden devices

Figure 5.1 – Chapter 5 Next Steps

Securing Your Brand

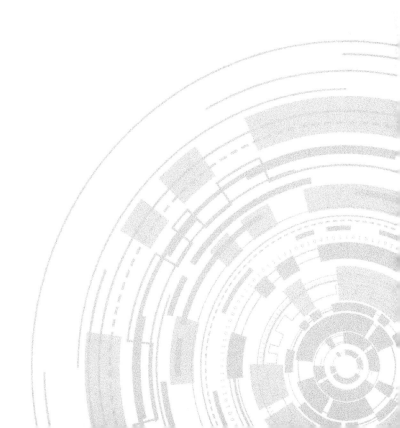

Introduction

Damage to your business can come in many forms. You can get robbed or fire can savage your shop, but perhaps the greatest damage is impact to your brand. Traditional insurance can reimburse you for theft and rebuild your burned-out shop. But recovering from brand damage is much more difficult.

Everything happens faster online. Going viral is great if mom's cookie recipe becomes an overnight international sensation. But the impact on your brand from a cyber incident can spread just as fast and have a devastating effect.

In Section 2, we're first going to talk about your online presence. Whether you have a company website or not, even if you think you have no online presence, you still have an online brand to manage, and security plays a major role in managing your online brand. Chapter 6 covers web and social media security.

After your online brand, we'll tackle data privacy in Chapter 7. Privacy is a hot topic, and I don't see that changing any time soon. People are still deciding what they want their public persona to mean to them. Whether that's about their latest post on social media, their latest online purchase, or their medical records, they want to know those records are safe and used the way they want them used. We must know how to keep their data safe. It is their data.

In Chapter 8, I'll demystify cyber insurance. More small businesses are choosing to carry cyber insurance, and it's a decision that each small business owner needs to make based on their specific circumstances. As you'll see from the case study presented in Chapter 7, not every company needs cyber insurance. After reading Chapter

8, you can decide for yourself based on the descriptions of the types of coverage and the questions you'll need to answer to apply.

Finally, in the Conclusion I'll summarize everything we've covered so you have a good action plan for turning these recommendations into the habits you will need to remain safe and secure online.

Chapter 6

Web and Social Media Security

With the advent of online commerce, first the Internet and then social media, the calculus hasn't changed about where or how to engage with your customers or potential customers. You want to be where your customers and prospects are and engage them in a way that gets your message across. The big difference is that what once was mostly a one-way, often static message has become a two-way dynamic dialog. Instead of advertising *to* your customers you are now engaging *with* your customers. Combining such factors as two-way or multi-party dialog and the democratization of ranking for companies and individuals has created both opportunity and risk. The upsides include better informing current and future customers and automating what were once completely manual processes, such as letting the prospect self-qualify. The downside is that these digital media come with security concerns and the potential for harm to reputation that must be managed.

Broadly speaking, you need to be aware of and manage your presence across these categories of digital assets:

- **Company website** – for small businesses, this is often a simple brochure site (describing products and services) or an eCommerce site (listing products for sale along with a shopping cart capability).

- **Social media sites** – such as Facebook, X/Twitter, LinkedIn, Instagram, TikTok, Threads, and YouTube.

- **Business listing or third-party review sites (TPRS)** – such as Yelp* For Business and Google My Business™.

- **E-commerce platforms** – such as Amazon, Etsy, and eBay.

- **Payment services** – such as Venmo, PayPal, and Square.

Given that new social media platforms seemingly pop up overnight and sometimes fall out of favor just as quickly, I will not try to review them all. However, around the time this book was published, Twitter changed its name to X and became a lightning rod for controversy. The behavior of high-profile users, including that of the service's owner, motivated other participants to alter their level of engagement on the site, including pulling back or discontinuing advertising and curtailing or stopping other forms of engagement, such as announcements and influencer activity. The point I am making is that you must remain diligent and continually evaluate where you choose to engage with your customers. While I don't expect another platform to fall from grace as quickly as X did, because things happen so quickly in the digital ecosystem the ROI calculation for money and time spent advertising and engaging on social media changes just as quickly.

In the following pages, I will go through the five categories listed above and describe the main risks you must be concerned with and the prudent steps you should consider.

Company Website

Whether or not you have your own company website or use a social media page as your primary digital presence, it should be driven by what is right for your business (and your customers). Don't assume you must have "mybusiness.com" or "mybusiness.biz" when it might be cheaper and more effective to use Facebook or Instagram, or even a Google My Business or Yelp* for Business page as your central online presence. If your business needs more customization than the social sites allow, there are a few risks you need to guard against. Whether choosing a website developer or working with your regular tech vendor, ask them to detail the security precautions they are taking and ensure you're getting a privately listed web domain with an SSL certificate. These are prudent security measures that don't cost much extra and are well worth the cost.

The next security issue to think about is how you interact on the site. If you want to provide an option for customers or prospects to fill out an input form or interact with you directly from your site, you must have data validation turned on to prevent fraudulent input. Your web firm or tech vendor can help with that.

Social Media Sites

As I mentioned above, it is not at all necessary for most small businesses to have their own website. Consider using one or more social media sites to create your desired online presence. The advantages are that the major social media companies are investing much more money than you could and have large staffs of highly trained individuals taking the necessary actions to operate safely and protect their platforms.

Whether you use a social media site as your central online presence or not, you will still probably need to engage with your customers and prospects using social media. Here is what you need to consider as you build your online presence.

Understanding the unique circumstances surrounding TikTok, which is majority owned by the Chinese company ByteDance, is also essential. TikTok's terms of service grant the app administrators extraordinary rights to access various types of sensitive data on the user's device. As a cybersecurity professional, I strongly recommend that you pass on using TikTok. As of this book's publication date, the U.S. Congress passed a bill that President Joe Biden signed that forces ByteDance to divest TikTok within nine months to a year so that the Chinese government does not control the app. Failing that, the federal government would ban TikTok in the United States. Additionally, as of this date, there are ongoing investigations of TikTok in Australia, the European Union, Turkey, and Canada.

1. Manage your password and access to your account.

Consistent with the advice in Chapters 4 and 5, you'll want to ensure you have strong passwords for your social media sites and have turned on two-factor authentication wherever possible.

If you have a lot of volume on the site and have one or more staff members acting as a proxy for you, it might be challenging to use two-factor authentication. If that's the case, make sure you coordinate changing your password with the people helping you and consider more frequent password changes than you would otherwise. This is another instance when using a password manager becomes very important. Several password managers allow you to automatically share certain passwords with specific people, which is a great way to automate managing access to your accounts.

Additionally, you'll want to use notification settings and act quickly when notified of an activity you didn't approve. It's also critical for both you and your staff to be vigilant for any unexpected posts from your account.

2. Consistently monitor all the social media sites where you have an account.

It is tempting to ignore or abandon sites that don't show much activity for you personally or your business. But if you abandon the account, it makes it a little easier for a thief to do an account takeover. Plus, you don't want to allow disparaging comments to go unchallenged. Be professional in your response; judgments are quick and harsh online. I recommend checking in and engaging daily on the platforms you use most, and weekly on those that drive less traffic for you.

3. **Apply the maximum privacy settings that don't interfere with your business.**

Remember the adage that if you are not paying for the product, you are the product. Social media sites offer a lot of free services. It is well known that they must sell something to make that model work. Yes, they sell ads, but they also sell you. By that, I mean they sell all the data you authorize them to sell. So, opt to turn the privacy setting on unless you really need the capability you are turning off.

4. **Use all the recovery options available to you.**

Social media sites offer various ways to recover access when you forget a password or get locked out. It can be difficult to regain access if this happens unless you can use one of their approved recovery options. These often take the form of alternative email accounts, recovery passwords, and alternate users who can access your account in case of a problem. I recommend setting up all such recovery options, especially for your high-traffic accounts.

Business Listings and Third-Party Review Sites (TPRS)

The main security issue with these sites is to claim your business.

Much like social media, you cannot completely control how your customers will find you, find out about you, or talk about you. You must claim your business on all the major sites. On most sites, there is a link or a button that asks, "Is this you?" or allows you to click to claim this as your business. This is not only prudent marketing best practice; you can avoid having bad actors disparage or exploit your good name by claiming your business. It is not uncommon for thieves to claim a company name with a good reputation and lure unsuspecting prospects to their scams. Claiming your business also allows you to provide consistent information across all platforms.

While not strictly a security issue, ensure you know how you are rated on each site and what those ratings mean. Just because the site provides a 5-point scale does not mean the average is 3. For some sites, anything less than 5 is judged negatively, and an average of around 4.7 starts to impact the types of customers sent your way.

One final point on this topic. Sometimes, you will receive a negative review and may be tempted to pay for a service to scrub your site. Be very careful with this. These services are generally scams, and the basic technique is to flood your company profile or products with positive reviews to push the negative reviews aside. This usually gets flagged as fraudulent, and you'll make the matter much worse.

The best approach is to be proactive and responsive but not reactive. Being proactive means asking for positive reviews when things go well and your customers are happy. This creates a bank of goodwill that can act as a buffer against negative reviews. Being responsive means addressing the negative reviews head-on but professionally. Engage with the reviewer if you can, try to make things right, and if you are able to correct the problem, ask for an update. Look carefully at the review itself, and if you think the review violates the TPRS's terms of service, file a complaint. The TPRS may remove it. Finally, don't be reactive, meaning, don't attack the reviewer or threaten legal action against the reviewer or the TPRS. Keep it professional, and you'll get better outcomes.

E-commerce Platforms and Payment Services

Treat e-commerce platforms and payment services as you would your bank. Turn on all security features, including two-factor authentication, extra control on money transfers, and appropriate notifications. You want to be alerted when money comes in (unless there is too much volume for you to appropriately monitor), especially when money is transferred from your payment platform to your bank, or checks are issued. Follow up on any unauthorized activity immediately.

E-commerce sites also act as TPRS's, allowing customers to leave reviews and ratings. These reviews and ratings are often critical to the selling process. I recommend the same approach—be proactive and encourage your happy customers to leave reviews so that the inevitable mishaps and unsatisfied customers won't disproportionately impact sales. Like a TPRS, some e-commerce sites allow for a company profile and allow you to link your profile to your main website. Venmo, for example, offers these features and others in a quest to create a community for data harvesting. Consider taking advantage of this feature for the same reasons described above, but ensure you have the privacy options locked down.

If you take payment cards through a point of sale (POS) terminal, whether a cash register or a smartphone, tablet, or PC running a payment app, make sure the service and your POS system are PCI compliant.

Figure 6.1 – Digital Engagement Platforms

In the next chapter, Data Privacy, we'll do a deep dive into privacy regulations, thresholds for credit cards, CCPA, and GDPR, and how they apply to you, but for now, here is a summary of the key steps we've covered to help you securely manage your social media presence.

Basic Steps

- Carefully manage who has the ability to access your social media accounts and act on your behalf
- Treat all payment services as you treat your bank, enable extra security, including two-factor authentication, and follow up on alerts

Intermediate Steps

- Monitor all of the major social media sites for activity about you and engage with clients and prospects as needed
- Claim your company on all business listings and third-party review sites (TPRS) so you can control the messaging and stop cyber-squatters from exploiting your good name
- Use a password manager to control who has access to your social media accounts, change the password often, and monitor all alerts

Pro Steps

- If you have a company website, upgrade to a web hosting plan that includes SSL security and security monitoring
- Apply the maximum privacy settings on your social media accounts and don't share data about you that doesn't benefit you and your business
- Develop a proactive social media engagement plan that routinely asks (but doesn't nag) for positive reviews to manage your ratings and create a buffer against poor reviews

Figure 6.2 – Chapter 6 Next Steps

As much as we'd all like to think rules and regulations are for larger companies, or at least other companies, it's hard to completely avoid them and still be in business. As a small business owner, you're subject to quite a few, including tax withholding and workplace safety. In addition, you could run into the PCI-DSS (Payment Card Industry Data Security Standard) depending on how you process credit cards for payment. And finally, there are state, federal, and international data privacy and breach notification laws. These also include the regulation known as CCPA (the California Consumer Privacy Act of 2018) and the 2020 amendment, the CPRA (the Consumer Privacy Rights Act).[3] In this chapter, we will go over the basics, including what these rules and regulations mean and how small companies can comply without hiring teams of lawyers and consultants.

Every State Has a Take

Besides the CCPA, which is intended to define California residents' rights over their data, every state in the U.S. has breach or privacy protection regulations.[4] All states have mandatory breach notification

---

[3] The CPRA amends the CCPA and does not create a separate new law. California therefore refers to the law as the CCPA or the CCPA as amended. I will use the same approach in this book.

[4] As of March 2018, when Alabama and South Dakota added protections. Prior to that, California introduced its breach notification law (SB 1386) in 2002, Nevada (N.R.S. § 603A) in 2005, Massachusetts (201 CMR 17) in 2009, and Texas (Texas Medical Records Privacy Act) in 2012. Each of these established key thresholds for compliance.

requirements that apply when defined criteria are met. Many states, like California, are establishing their own privacy regulations, most with expectations for "reasonable" security.[5] The CCPA is different; it includes far more extensive privacy rights for consumers (referred to as data subjects) over how their data is used and what data is covered. These are significant differences, as we'll see a little later. Although California is only one state, it is often on the forefront of consumer protection and other states are likely to base their next generation of rules at least partially on the California model. So, I think it's worth a little discussion.

The point of privacy breach notification laws is to require companies to disclose when customer or consumer data has been inappropriately accessed and, by way of the requirements and subsequent penalties for failure to comply, force companies to take proper measures to secure personal data.

I mentioned above that CCPA differs slightly from the other state and federal regulations. The CCPA goes beyond breach notification and establishes data protection regulations. It also endows citizens (consumers) with rights over their data, while the predecessor state regulations were conceived as merely protections to prevent harm to citizens. These rights include the right to not have your data collected, the right to obtain a copy of the data a company holds about you, and the right to have that data deleted by the company.

The CCPA uses an opt-out model (consumers can opt out of data collection campaigns and the sale of their data as opposed to an opt-in model that requires a company to get permission before collecting data), which is typical in the U.S., and establishes the right that California residents be informed regarding the nature of the information collected about them and the source of this information.

---

[5]   Typically, there are safe harbor provisions for encrypted data, but many of the privacy regulations require entities holding consumer data to take reasonable measures to ensure the security of that data.

The CCPA also establishes the notion of non-discrimination when consumers exercise their privacy rights.

The Banks Got in the Act as Well

While all the states were sewing together their patchwork quilt of data privacy laws, in 2004 the payment card industry put the Payment Card Industry Data Security Standard (PCI-DSS) in place because payment card fraud had been increasing at an alarming rate. Sadly, we're not even close to out of the woods. Credit card fraud is still a multi-billion-dollar problem.

What Applies to You?

The first issue you must worry about is whether you trigger the various thresholds for compliance. In the chart labeled Figure 7.1, I've put together some general guidelines. This is a good rule-of-thumb guide but does not substitute for legal advice. If you're not sure you should, at a minimum, read the regulations for your locale. You might also want to consult a lawyer specializing in consumer data privacy.

These compliance requirements have a lot in common. They all aim to protect private consumer (citizen) data, and they all come with associated reporting, penalties (including possible fines) for non-compliance, and various types of enforcement. From a data security perspective, they have similar requirements for how to comply. They mainly differ in the specifics of what happens when a breach occurs.

These differences include thresholds for what constitutes a reportable event, how quickly the event must be reported, under what circumstances the individual consumers must be notified vs. the regulator, what restitution is owed to the consumer, and what fine or other sanction might be levied by regulators.

How do the regulations apply to your business?						
Privacy Trigger	**If**	**Then**	**If**	**Then**	**If**	**Then**
Credit Cards	No annual credit card transactions	No PCI-DSS compliance requirements	1-20,000 annual credit card transactions	PCI Level 4 compliance required	20,000 - 1,000,000 annual credit card transactions	PCI level 3 compliance required
Medical Records	• Do not provide healthcare services • Do not provide services that access PHI for a covered entity	No HIPAA compliance requirements	Healthcare provider (Covered Entity)	HIPAA compliance required	Provide services to healthcare provider (Business Associate)	HIPAA compliance required
Personal Information about Consumers	Collect data on resident of any state	Potentially subject to the data privacy laws of the state	Consult a reference such as this one: https://www.mintz.com/mintz-matrix that lists thresholds and requirements for every state.			
Personal Information about Californians	Processes personal information of 50,000 or fewer consumers, households, or devices	CCPA compliance not required	>50,000 annual credit card transactions or more than $25M in annual revenue	CCPA compliance required	50% or more of business activity involves personal data	CCPA compliance required
Personal Information about EU Citizens	• No presence in an EU country • Have <250 employees	No GDPR compliance requirements	A presence in an EU country	GDPR compliance requirement	• Process personal data of EU residents • Have >250 employees	GDPR compliance requirement

Figure 7.1 – How the Regulations Apply to Your Business

Here is a case study that profiles a small business, an electrolysis service and bridal store, and shows how they comply with their obligations.

CASE STUDY

Company Profile

Electrolysis practice and bridal store

Background and Cybersecurity/Data Privacy Issues

This is both a personal services (electrolysis) business and a retail (bridal store) business. As such, the proprietor must comply with a larger superset of regulations. Because the electrolysis business is not considered a health care provider, it does not fall under HIPAA. Both businesses take credit cards and debit cards, and they operate in the state of California, so they do potentially fall under CCPA. They use both payment apps on mobile devices for the electrolysis services and a Point of Sale (POS) terminal in the bridal shop. While this book is being written, combating the COVID-19 pandemic is causing many businesses to implement various personal safety measures.

Solutions That Work

- Routinely follows the CA State Board of Barbering and Cosmetology for guidance about safely providing services to consumers.

- Works with their bank and their payment system vendor to understand what they should do to safeguard payment card data, including any updates to procedures.

- When choosing their bank and their payment system, they specifically limited their selection to those that provided solutions that were PCI compliant.

- Chose not to carry cyber insurance as they do not retain customer records with sensitive data, and they do not retain payment card information in their office.

What They Would Do If an Incident Occurred

If a cyber incident occurred, they would call their local law enforcement, their bank, and their payment system vendor.

Figure 7.2 – Electrolysis Service and Bridal Store Case Study

How to Comply

The second issue you need to worry about is how to comply. The chart in Figure 7.3 shows a checklist you should apply to your operations.

Compliance Level	Requirements to Comply
Level 3 PCI	Complete Annual Self-Assessment Questionnaire
	Conduct Quarterly Scans
	Provide Validated Submission
Level 4 PCI	Complete Annual Self-Assessment Questionnaire
	Conduct Quarterly Scans
HIPAA	Adhere to the HIPAA Privacy and Security Rules
	Execute Business Associate Agreements with any third party with whom the organization shares PHI
CCPA	Implement the Micro-Business Compliance Checklist
GPDR	Implement the Micro-Business Compliance Checklist

Figure 7.3 – Compliance Checklist

Don't be intimidated by these requirements. A self-assessment questionnaire simply requires you to review the status of your payment card protections and self-report which controls are in place and which you may be working to implement. Your point-of-sale vendor or bank can help you pick the proper questionnaire and answer any questions you are unsure of. Quarterly scans and validated submissions are typically done for you by your merchant service. I highly recommend that micro-businesses outsource web-based payment processing to a PCI-compliant service provider.

PCI Requirements for Level 4 and Level 3 Merchants

You can see from Figure 7.3 how the advice I have provided throughout this book translates to the formal PCI requirements.

Controls You Can Count On

After the PCI requirements, the next two graphics list the controls I've described throughout this book (Figure 7.4 – Micro-Business Control Set) and the steps you would take to comply with data privacy and protection regulations based on your situation, as set forth in Figure 7.1 (Figure 7.5 – Micro-Business Compliance Checklist).

Goals	PCI DSS Requirements
Build and Maintain a Secure Network and Systems	1. Install and maintain a firewall configuration to protect cardholder data 2. Do not use vendor-supplied defaults for system passwords and other security parameters
Protect Cardholder Data	3. Protect cardholder data 4. Encrypt transmission of cardholder data across open, public networks
Maintain a Vulnerability Management Program	5. Protect all systems against malware and regularly update anti-virus software or programs 6. Develop and maintain secure systems and applications
Implement Strong Access Control Measures	7. Restrict access to cardholder data by business need to know 8. Identify and authenticate access to system components 9. Restrict physical access to cardholder data
Regularly Monitor and Test Networks	10. Track and monitor all access to network resources and cardholder data 11. Regularly test security systems and processes
Maintain an Information Security Policy	12. Maintain a policy that addresses information security for all personnel

Figure 7.4 – PCI DSS Requirements

Micro-Business Control Set

- Put important papers in locked drawers

- Secure your bank accounts by limiting or removing wire transfer capabilities

- Make sure all money movement requires a second verification step

- Implement a cybersecurity training program for all employees

- Change default passwords

- Install and use a firewall and anti-malware software

- Configure your routers and WiFi routers with advanced settings to restrict use outside your network

- Apply updates for perimeter and network devices as soon as they are available

- Implement a 3-2-1 backup strategy using a backup solution that automates daily, weekly and monthly backup processes

- Assign every employee their own unique account

- Limit the number of people with privileged or administrator accounts to people with a need to know

- Disable all unused system accounts

- Use unique passwords for all accounts, no exceptions, including social media and all online services

- Use restrictive privacy settings for all online services

- Turn on broad notifications for all financial and customer engagement activity

Figure 7.5 – Micro-Business Control Set

Micro-Business Compliance Checklist

1. Document the personal data that you hold, where it came from, and who you share it with.

2. Review how you seek, record, and manage consent, and whether you need to make any changes.

3. Consider how you will verify individuals' ages and how to obtain parental or guardian consent when needed for any data processing activity.

4. Create and document a procedure to provide an individual for whom you hold personal data a complete data set in a commonly readable format such as MS Word document, Google Doc, Excel spreadsheet, CSV file, or PDF file within 30 days of a request.

5. Create and document a procedure to delete all data you hold (except that which you are legally required to keep, such as PHI and tax related data) on any individual within 30 days, should a request be made.

6. Verify you have procedures in place to detect, report, and investigate a personal data breach.

7. Implement the micro-business control set defined above.

8. Review your current privacy disclosures and make any necessary changes.

9. Train your employees to protect personal information, to observe and report inappropriate access to personal information, and to understand their obligations under the regulations.

10. Create a list of parties you will notify in the case of a breach, whether you discover it, or it is reported to you by a service provider. Include at a minimum your insurance agent, your lawyer, law enforcement (working with your lawyer), your bank (or the provider of your merchant services) and the appropriate state authorities.

Specific to the CCPA
1. Create a clear and conspicuous homepage privacy link.

Specific to the GDPR
1. Identify the lawful basis for your processing activity and document it.

Figure 7.6 – Micro-Business Compliance Checklist

Privacy Disclosures

As I mentioned, the state of California has a long history of consumer protection regulations. Because California accounts for an outsized percentage of the U.S. economy, California regulations tend to get outsized attention and policy often follows suit. If you have customers in California, pay close attention to the requirements for privacy disclosures for the CCPA. They are specific. It is also possible similar regulations will come into existence in other states, so being familiar with the CCPA can help you be prepared.

The CCPA gives consumers the right to know exactly what personal information is being collected about them and the sources of this information. To comply with this law, businesses must provide a disclosure before they collect the information. The disclosure must inform consumers about the categories of personal information being collected and the purposes for which the personal information will be used. You must also disclose where that personal information is gathered from, the categories of third parties with whom it is shared, and any specific pieces of personal information collected. Work with your tech vendor or website developer to create the proper disclosure.

If you do business in more than one state or have customers from other states, we strongly recommend that you work with a privacy law firm that is versed in privacy laws for those states. This firm can help you refine your checklist, meet your initial reporting deadlines, and advise on which authorities to notify and when.

This means you must take the precautions your bank and insurance company recommend, implement the controls suggested in Chapters 1 through 7, and ensure that your employees understand their responsibilities and act accordingly.

Resources

- The official **CCPA** site:
  https://oag.ca.gov/privacy/ccpa
- A list of **state privacy legislation** (as of the printing of this book):
  https://en.wikipedia.org/wiki/State_privacy_laws_of_the_United_States
- **Web content accessibility guidelines:**
  (WCAG)https://www.w3.org/WAI/standards-guidelines/wcag/

In the next chapter, Cyber Insurance, I'll provide a primer on cyber insurance, including what it covers, what it doesn't cover, when you should get it, and what you need to do to qualify. But for now, here is a summary of the key steps we've covered to help you guard your payment card data, and comply with state privacy and breach notification laws.

Basic Steps

- Review Figure 7.1 and determine how PCI, HIPAA, CCPA, and the GDPR apply to you

- Make a list of all the states where you do business, or where your customers reside

- Update your privacy notifications and disclosures to meet minimum disclosure requirements

Intermediate Steps

- Make a list of all the personal information you collect on your customers, where you get it, how you use it, and who you share it with

- Meet with a privacy lawyer and map out a notification checklist in the event of a breach of personal data you maintain

Pro Steps

- Prepare for the eventual nation-wide rollout of legislation similar to the CCPA by implementing the micro-business compliance checklist

Figure 7.7 – Chapter 7 Next Steps

If you're interested in additional background, here are the regulations from the trailblazing states:

Key Provisions in a Nutshell

State	Key Provision	Details
California	Breach notification	When published in 2002, SB 1386 provided the first set of state breach notification rules.
		https://en.wikipedia.org/wiki/California_S.B._1386
Massachusetts	Preventive controls requirements	201 CMR 17 raised the compliance bar in 2009 by establishing minimum standards that companies were required to take to try to prevent potential breaches.
		https://en.wikipedia.org/wiki/201_CMR_17.00 https://www.mass.gov/files/documents/2017/11/21/compliance-checklist.pdf
Nevada	More breach notification requirements	Published in 2005, these breach notification rules expanded on the California requirements, notably by requiring encryption for sensitive information.
		https://en.wikipedia.org/wiki/State_privacy_laws_of_the_United_States#Nevada
Texas	Medical records privacy	Texas set broader requirements so that more companies fell under the rules for notification about medical records leaks in 2012 when it passed the Texas Medical Records Privacy Act.
		https://texaslawhelp.org/article/state-and-federal-health-privacy-laws

Figure 7.8 – Key Provisions

Chapter 8

Cyber Insurance

Cyber insurance is one of the fastest-growing segments of insurance for small businesses. The reasons won't surprise you. The most significant drivers are that more companies are demanding cyber insurance as a requirement for doing business, and the increasing incidence of cybercrime against small businesses.

Insurance is a risk management tool, period. It is not a moral decision; we're not good or bad if we do or don't carry insurance. Whether or not you get cyber insurance (or any insurance for that matter) for your company should be a decision you come to after weighing the risks of adverse events (for example, the likelihood and impact of inappropriate disclosure or losing a contract) against the cost of the premiums for the coverage obtained.

What Cyber Insurance Covers

Cyber insurance protects the policy holder from losses from cyber incidents. Cyber insurance covers two distinct expense categories: first-party expenses (the policy holder's specific expenses) and third-party claims (the exposure to claims against the policy holder given a breach or other such incident).

First-party expense coverage is designed to cover expenses tied directly to the policy holder, including cyber extortion, business interruption, and other business-related expenses associated with the breach. The latter includes items such as digital forensics costs (typically very expensive) and costs associated with breach response (e.g., customer notifications and credit monitoring services).

Third-party expense coverage addresses penalties and regulatory actions related to privacy and security violations resulting from the inadequate privacy and security protections of the policy holder. Third-party coverage may also include content-related issues, including copyright infringements, libel, and slander. Policies generally have coverage limits, with sub-limits for specific first-party and third-party damage.

The types of cyber incidents fall into three categories:

Category One – Probably the most easily understood is the loss due to the inappropriate disclosure of private or protected information. This is typically called a data breach, and while that sounds like a bad actor is involved, this category also covers unintentional breaches, such as sending sensitive information to the wrong customer. Coverage in these cases includes all or part of the costs to notify the people who are the subjects of the breach, state or other regulatory fines, the cost of breach remediation, including fixing systems and providing identity monitoring, and in some cases, losses due to systems being offline while being remediated—effectively business interruption coverage.

Category Two – Probably the most common for micro-businesses, this category includes business email compromise (BEC) and malware attacks (often but not always delivered via email) such as ransomware and crypto mining. Some insurance carriers call this entire category BEC. However, I prefer to distinguish between BEC and phishing attacks because learning to avoid each type of attack is different. Coverage in this case might include the cost of scrubbing malware from your systems, recovering money lost, and possibly even paying the ransom. The latter is a decision your insurance carrier would make with you depending on the cost of recovering versus the likelihood that the cyber thieves would be willing and able to give you the unlock key. Many insurance companies are now brokering the payments and serving as intermediaries negotiating the ransom.

It is a good idea to ask your agent whether this service is included. You'll want to read the pertinent contract language carefully each time you renew your policy as federal law evolves regarding payments to criminals, especially criminals residing in countries currently sanctioned by the U.S. Government.

<u>Category Three</u> – Includes protection against fines and judgments because content you are responsible for, such as information or dialog posted on a company website or attributed to you on some system accessible on the Internet, becomes a matter of dispute. This would include information that is controversial in some way, such as offensive content or content that is claimed as the intellectual property of another party. Depending on your policy, this might also include protection for advertising and statements made public to promote your business that might infringe on the rights of others. In this case, coverage might include lawyer's fees and judgments awarded in compensation to the aggrieved party.

While these are the general categories of risk that a small business cyber policy might cover, they are also the categories of risk that drive cost. So, for instance, if you are required to have cyber insurance and your carrier determines your risk in those three categories is low, they may charge a lot less for the policy. Conversely, the more risk in each category, the higher your premiums.

Determining Risk

The insurer will perform a risk assessment to determine your risk exposure. This is usually done (at least initially) with an intake form that asks questions about your business activities and cyber hygiene practices. In some cases, the carrier may want to visit you to thoroughly assess your risk of loss.

First up is usually general information about your company. The carrier would want to know the name and address of the business and the nature of the products and services provided. Specific industries are subject to more cyber activity than others. Additional demographic information is requested, such as number of employees, revenue, and gross profit. This is common to the general liability questionnaire if you've considered such coverage.

In addition to the general information, there are usually questions to help identify sources of risk. You'll likely be asked if you collect credit card information or personal information.

You'll also be asked about specific measures you take to protect your systems, such as backups, encryption, and endpoint protection. Additionally, the carrier will want to know how you protect your business legally by asking, for instance, if all customers sign a contract (along with specific terms) and if you conduct background checks on prospective employees.

Every carrier has a list of procedures they require you to have before they underwrite a policy for you. Common across most carriers are backups and endpoint protection. Most will add encryption of sensitive data if you collect and store credit card data. I recommend that you work with your tech vendor to answer these questions and use that as an opportunity to discuss which additional security measures you should have in place.

The last category of information the carrier would collect is your loss history. This, again, is common to your general liability policy. They will want to know if you have had a payout for a cyber incident within the last three years. And, of course, they all ask if you are aware of any issue that would cause a payout. They want to know if you are trying to close the proverbial barn door after the horses have left.

Another key element you need to be aware of is the exclusions in your policy. Some policies may exclude coverage for losses arising from shortcomings in your security program, usually if you were aware of these shortcomings before purchasing the policy or failed to take reasonable care. Ensure you know what is required to document that you are taking prudent action. Record your hygiene activities to show you were taking reasonable care. Most policies will also have exclusions for acts of terrorism or war. It's tempting to think this will not apply to you as you are not likely to be the victim of a nation-state or a terrorist organization, but collateral damage from these events can impact you if you also rely on the systems or infrastructure that are damaged. So, just be aware of this before you execute your policy.

Whether or not you can obtain the coverage you want will ultimately depend on the risk you present to the carrier. This will be determined by assessing the business you are in and the way you conduct your business. If you deal with payment card information, for example, and do not take adequate steps to secure this information, you will likely be denied coverage until you can correct the deficiencies. As you've probably already figured out, implementing the micro-business control set and applying the micro-business compliance checklist defined in Chapter 7 are the actions I recommend you take to make qualifying for cyber liability insurance more likely. Keep records of your compliance activities to demonstrate your due care to the carrier.

Finally, keep in mind that different insurance carriers have different risk tolerance and differing levels of experience underwriting cyber insurance. Shop around. Interview the broker as they are interviewing you. Make sure that the broker is an expert in cyber insurance. These are still relatively new policies relative to insurance in general. Do your homework.

In the Conclusion, I'm going to summarize what we've covered in this book and recommend ways of readying yourself for a future event, but for now, here is a summary of the key steps I've covered to help you be an intelligent cyber insurance consumer and take the actions to keep losses and premiums at a minimum.

Basic Steps

- Determine whether you need cyber insurance (e.g., due to contractual needs or driven by your high-risk activities)
- If cyber insurance is a contractual requirement, verify your minimum coverages

Intermediate Steps

- Implement the micro-business control set
- Comparison shop with two or more carriers
- Interview the insurance agent as they evaluate you

Pro Steps

- Apply the micro-business compliance checklist
- Review checklist and control set records annually with your carrier and reevaluate premiums based on loss history and the safeguards you have in place

Figure 8.1 – Chapter 8 Next Steps

I dedicated this book to all the entrepreneurs who have entered the arena with a dream of greatness and a will to make it happen. You know what it means to own every problem. I hope this book helps you rest a little easier when it comes to securing your business in the digital marketplace.

There are a few steps I recommend you repeat periodically so that you can deal with any cyber incident that comes your way. This advice comes primarily from the Pro Steps I've outlined throughout the book. You'll also see the pattern—routine! Develop routines around cyber safety. Just as personal hygiene depends on routine, so too does cyber hygiene.

- Routinely check the office and make sure you have not become lax in locking things up. When devices aren't in use, when you're done with your paperwork, when no one is in the shop—lock it up.

- Check your email and your smartphone for notifications from your bank. Make sure that you are following up on any suspicious activity.

- Review one of the recommended publications from Chapter 2 each week. Stay up on the developments in the cybercrime world.

- Hold monthly or quarterly lunches with your employees and use the opportunity to learn what they are experiencing. Have they seen anything happen that you need to be aware of? Are they remaining diligent? The number one attack vector for small businesses (all businesses really) is email. No clicking on unexpected attachments or responding to emergencies without verifying that they are real.

- Routinely test your backups. Nothing is more frustrating than dead batteries in the flashlight when the power goes out and nothing is more destructive to your business than not having a good backup when something happens to your data.

- Don't let your guard down when you are traveling. Use a VPN to access the Internet if possible and bring your own battery backup so that you are never plugging your device into a public charging station. Make sure you always sweep your hotel room, coffee shop, and Airbnb for hidden devices.

- Routinely validate who has access to your applications and ensure than they are still on your team and the access they have lines up with the role they play.

- Keep up on what customers are saying on social media and stay engaged. The old adage that the best defense is a good offense is never more apt than on social media.

- Routinely check the privacy settings for social media. The social media sites are selling data, data about you. They are constantly adding more engagement features and each feature comes with its own privacy settings. Minimize data leakage by checking the settings periodically.

- Stay aware of the advances in privacy legislation. Privacy is at the forefront of consumer protection now that our lives are so intertwined with technology. The news sources I listed in Chapter 2 will be covering privacy developments and you should use those publications to stay informed and be proactive, so the privacy expectations of your customers don't pass you by.

- On an annual basis, review your notification checklist with your privacy lawyer and your insurance broker.

- In case of a cybersecurity incident, keep the list of "in the event of emergency" contacts up to date and include law enforcement on that list. Go to https://www.ready.gov/cybersecurity, which is the site maintained by the U.S. Department of Homeland Security. Steps to take after a breach can be found in Appendix A of this book.

For those of you who are experiencing significant growth, this book might serve as a primer, but you may find yourself needing more concrete steps you can take to take your cybersecurity program to the next level. In that case, I highly recommend another book in the CISO Desk Reference Guide catalog that is geared toward slightly larger companies with a need for a more mature program. Alan Watkins' book *Creating a Small Business Cybersecurity Program* takes you step-by-step through the process of creating a formal, structured program that will help you get to that next level.

OK, there you have it. You are now ready to keep your business secure.

Appendix A – Ready.Gov Cybersecurity Page

https://www.ready.gov/cybersecurity

Here is an excerpt taken from this site and then modified with additional recommendations.

After a Cyberattack

- Contact your insurance agent if you have a cybersecurity insurance policy or rider.

- File a report with the Office of the Inspector General (OIG) if you think someone is illegally using your Social Security number. (https://www.idtheft.gov/)

- File a complaint with the FBI Internet Crime Complaint Center (IC3). They will review the complaint and refer it to the appropriate agency. (https://www.ic3.gov/)

- File a report with the local police so there is an official record of the incident.

- Report identity theft to the Federal Trade Commission. (http://www.ftc.gov/)

- Contact additional agencies depending on what information was stolen. Examples include contacting the Social Security Administration (800-269-0271) if your social security number was compromised, or the Department of Motor Vehicles if your driver's license or car registration has been stolen. (http://oig.ssa.gov/report)

- Report online crime or fraud to your local United States Secret Service (USSS) Electronic Crimes Task Force (http://www.secretservice.gov/investigation/#field) or the Internet Crime Complaint Center.

- For further information on preventing and identifying threats, visit US-CERT's Alerts and Tips page. (http://www.us-cert.gov/alerts-and-tips/)

Bill Bonney is a security evangelist, author, and consultant. As co-author of the Cybersecurity Canon Hall of Fame two-volume *CISO Desk Reference Guide*, Bill and co-authors Matt Stamper and Gary Hayslip are dedicated to providing the practical advice needed to combat the ongoing scourge of cybercrime. Prior to co-founding CISO DRG Publishing, Bill was Vice President of Product Marketing and Chief Strategist at UBIQ (formerly FHOOSH), a maker of high-speed encryption software; Vice President of Product Marketing and Principal Consulting Analyst at TechVision Research; and Director of Information Security and Compliance at Intuit, maker of personal and small business financial products.

Bill holds multiple patents in data protection, access, and classification, and was an early member of the Board of Advisors for CyberTECH, a San Diego incubator. He was a founding member of the board of directors for the San Diego CISO Round Table, a professional group focused on building relationships and fostering collaboration in information security management. Bill is a highly regarded speaker and panelist addressing technology and security concerns. He holds a Bachelor of Science degree in Computer Science and Applied Mathematics from Albany University.

LinkedIn Profile: https://www.linkedin.com/in/billbonney

David Goodman is a consultant working in digital transformation, specifically the areas of identity management and security, data protection and privacy regulation as well as emerging technologies. He has worked in senior management positions across a wide range of companies in Europe and North America, from start-ups (Soft-Switch, Metamerge) to global brands (Lotus Development, IBM, Nokia Siemens Networks and Ericsson) as well as University College London. David is currently a principal consulting analyst with TechVision Research, chief evangelist with iGrant.io, a senior consultant with Trust in Digital Life association and, until recently, executive director of the Open Identity Exchange (OIX). He is work package leader for dissemination and communication in the CyberSec4Europe and CSI-COP H2020 projects, and task leader for Open Banking roadmapping and demonstrators in CyberSec4Europe. David has a BA from the University of Manchester and a D.Phil. from the Oriental Institute, University of Oxford.

LinkedIn Profile: https://www.linkedin.com/in/david275/
https://identitas.consulting/